HOW TO DEVELOP PERSONALITY

HOW TO DEVELOP PERSONALITY

RAJAN KUMAR

ISBN 979-888606513-8

this book mainly dedicated to people who want to devlop ther personility and want to look different amongthe people

Contents

Part 1

Foreword

THIS BOOK HELP THE YOUNG PEOPLE AS WEEL AS TO THE PEOPLE WHO WANT TO DEVELOPE THIRE PERSONILITY. SPECIALLY THIS BOOK IS WRITTEN FOR PEOPLE WHO WANT TO GET SUCESS IN THERE LIFE AND ACHIEVE THER GOALS AS RESULT THE MAIN PROBLEMS THAT PEOPLE FACE DURING THER INTERVIEW IS PERSONILITY.SO THIS BOOK IS GOING TO HELP THEV PEOPLE.

Preface

THE OBJECTIVE AND THE AIM OF THE BOOK IS TO HELP THE PEOPLE WHO WANT TO GET SUCESS IN THERE LIFE .BUT THEY DONT KNOW HOW TO DO SO THIS BOOK IS GOING TO HELP AND SUPPORT THEM .

Acknowledgements

THIS BOOK IS WRITTEN ON SOURCES EXPERT AND WEB WHICH GOING TO HELP AND CHANGE THE LIFE OF MANY PEOPLE

Prologue

WHAT IS PERSONILITY ,HOW TO DEVELOPE IT ,HOW TO BECOME THE SUCESS PEOPLE ALL THIS QUESTION SOLUTIONARE IN THIS BOOK

How to develpe the personility.and look different among the people this book help the people to loook different compare to other.or normal people

WELCOME TO THE JOURNEY OF PERSONILITY .WHICH GOING TO HELP YOU HOW TO BE A SUCESS AN
THROUGH THE HELP OF THIS BOOK

WE HOPE THAT YOU PEOPLE GOT TO KNOW WHY PERSONILITY IS IMPOTANT NOWDAYS AND HOW TO BE A
SUCESS PEOPLE THROUGH THE PERSONILITY